REQUIEM IN RHYME

VOLUME 2

SERIES: REQUIEM IN RHYME

REQUIEM IN RHYME
VOLUME 2

Emotional Boogaloo

DUSTIN EDWARDS

Columbus, Ohio

The views and opinions expressed in this book are solely those of the author and do not reflect the views or opinions of Gatekeeper Press. Gatekeeper Press is not to be held responsible for and expressly disclaims responsibility of the content herein.

REQUIEM IN RHYME
Emotional Boogaloo

Published by **Gatekeeper Press**
2167 Stringtown Rd, Suite 109
Columbus, OH 43123-2989
www.GatekeeperPress.com

Copyright © 2022 by **Dustin Edwards**

All rights reserved. Neither this book, nor any parts within it may be sold or reproduced in any form or by any electronic or mechanical means, including information storage and retrieval systems, without permission in writing from the author. The only exception is by a reviewer, who may quote short excerpts in a review.

The editorial work for this book is entirely the product of the author. Gatekeeper Press did not participate in and is not responsible for any aspect of this element.

Copyright for the image:
iStockphoto.com/4FR *(lake Shore hiding in fog)*

Library of Congress Control Number: 2022931662

ISBN (hardcover):
ISBN (paperback): 9781662928987
eISBN: 9781662928994

FOREWORD

I have no idea what the fuck I'm doing.

Whether or not I have any business being here is yet to be determined. ... But this isn't about me.

I've known Dustin for many years now. Not as well as some, better than most, though, for sure.

We used to work together in a restaurant. That seems like a lifetime ago now. I think that says a lot about him. How many people have you worked with to date? How many of those people would you consider true friends? For me, not many, to be sure. But Dustin is one of them. I think that speaks volumes to his character. To come out of an environment remaining friends when most coworker relationships are fleeting at best is rather remarkable.

We've been through some things together. From late night video games and a bottle of scotch, to an NFL game in NYC in cold rain. to an early morning phone call when he was in need of some help. Dustin has been through things that the vast majority of us couldn't begin to fathom, and emerged to enlighten us. Of the many thoughts I've had in attempts to suss him out over the years, one rings truer to me than most. Dustin wants us all to be better human beings.

Dustin is nothing if he's not honest. Sometimes that honesty can be brash, or make us uncomfortable, but at the end of the day we all have room to grow, to be better human beings. Certain degrees of discomfort, in the proper instances, help us grow as people. And I've felt that that's all Dustin's ever wanted from others. Honesty. And decency. From and for everyone. He's inspired me to be a better person, to be a better father, to be a better husband, to be more considerate of others, knowing full well that I have no idea what they're going through at any given moment. For that I'll always be thankful and hold him in high regard.

I'm not good at many things, but I do genuinely believe, as objectively as one can be in a thought such as this, to be a good judge of character. I believe that Dustin is one of the best of us. So, while I'm certain this isn't exactly what he's looking for in a foreword, this is what he gets. This is what he deserves.

I'm honored that he asked me to write this. More than he'll ever know. And I'm grateful he's not only found a medium to share himself with us, but a vehicle in which to share it widely. I hope you, reader, find inspiration to do the same.

Dustin, I love you, man. And I'm glad you're here.

-OG

CONTENTS

Broken aka the Oliver Special	8
Accidental Laugh	9
Ozzymandias	10
Apology Flex	11
Be Authentic	12
Be Good to People	13
Benevolence	14
Care about grey matter	15
Blank Space	16
Caged Up	18
Call Me Tomorrow	19
Canary Tales	20
Confessional	21
Conversation	22
Court Session	23
Curse Well	24
Cuts Deep	25
Demonology	26
Distinct God	28
Doctor Strange Love	29

Dopamine Shot	30	*Laugh Randomly*	56
Dumb it down	32	*Lightning and Thunder*	58
Dumb Kid	34	*Liquid*	59
Fast Food for My Soul	35	*Little Talk*	60
Feel Free to Laugh at My Inanity	36	*Lullaby for the End of the World*	62
Dry for a While	38	*Manipulate and Modulate*	64
Greed	39	*Mental Illness on a Page*	65
GTFO	40	*Mental Mansion*	66
Here They Are	41	*Metronome*	67
Heaven and Hell	42	*Needless War*	68
Hold My Tongue	44	*Nonsense Now*	70
Human a Bit Better	45	*Nothing to Say*	71
Ain't Never Would	46	*Odd State Horror Story*	72
I Am broken	48	*Open Your Eyes*	73
I Am Legitimately Not Giving This Poem a Title	50	*Outer Space*	74
Missed Chef's Kiss	52	*Putting in the Work*	75
If you only knew	53	*Reflection Averse*	76
Know Or Don't	54	*Refraction*	77
		Scared For No Reason	78

Scorn	79	*We the People*	111
Side Gig	80	*Wall Street Gangs*	112
Staying Alive	81	*Write the Tears Away*	114
Slay Demons	82	*Word Stew*	116
Snacks	84	*Over the Hill*	117
Stay in Your Lane	86		
Still Us	88		
Stringing Lexical Bricks	90		
Surgeon	92		
Take Care of Each Other	93		
The Devil Doesn't Want Me	94		
Thinking	95		
The Interview	96		
The One Where He Writes TV Jokes	102		
This One's for the Nerds	104		
Throw Words	106		
Trained to Grey	108		
Trigonometry	109		
Uncomfortably Good	110		

Broken aka the Oliver Special _____

"It's what we do with our broken that matters"
How we sweep and mop up the glass when it shatters
How we handle all the heart pitter patters
How we handle all the spills and splatters
How we handle all the clothes shred to tatters

This one goes out to a real OG
Without that man, I wouldn't be me
Hell, without that man, I wouldn't even be

That quote is his, I'll always owe him
Staring death in the face, this dude, I phoned him
Whilst losing my breath, he helped postpone me

We do what we can, for those who cannot
Because most people don't, and others are caught
Sipping their coffee, or their cup of tea
Reading the paper thinking me, me, me

While black men are shot
Children are bought
And so many have naught
Cause of some prick on a yacht

I use my broken to send a message
All humans have purpose
You will not usurp us
Good people, true surplus
Real people, truth surplus

"It's what we do with our broken that matters"
Not petty social media chatter
Or how pretty the food on your platter
Or the number of people you flatter

Accidental Laugh _____

Funny on accident, a brain mostly not society fit
Then amusing on purpose to distract it a bit
Don't get me wrong, roll intellect bonus, that's wit
Work word magic, casting it all with each spit

Literary nerd jokes if you haven't caught on
I never log out, a broken cranium is never not on
Even with a chance card, you couldn't stop on
The monopoly, I've earned $200 and passed, so Go on

Wealth is a broken, top-down system
Didn't get rid of slavery, just an owner system
Cash a check, cast a vote, owned by a system
Only the systems decide that we need a system

To tell me I'm wrong, you'd need a shot in the arm
Argument trumped, so you're triggered, fake harm
No one's A'Biden so you can't sound the alarm
I'm just here with a sidearm and charm

I have bad days when I abhor myself and hate you too
There's not a lot of metaphor in this, my head is a zoo
That's when I absorb happy vibes from others on cue
Because I've never been able to change my own view

I hate my own name
I hate my own breath
I hate that I'm insane
I hate that I seem to elude death

I love people more than the beat of my own heart
I love my own failure, but I'm not afraid to own my art
I love every single person from here to Musk's Mars
I love every single person that hates all of my bars

Ozzymandias

Know what you want 'til you get it
Talk a big game but can't spit it
Fast ball behind the helmet, can't hit it
I'll use words so well that you quit it

Retire from it early, you'll know why I came
Not like your dad, don't have your last name
Fame is lame, just here for perspectives in frame
Plaque for acclaim. People know pen game from nickname

I own every misdeed in my own account
Not a single thing I've done I want to discount
But my lack of head count is no paramount
If not, there doesn't exist my sermon on the mount

So here are my words, I will say them gently
Love a bunch of people, and do it intently
If you must screw it up, understand it consequently
That's a poor use of English, but I did incidentally

There's not a being on Earth to negate my love
No deity can argue, below or above
That empathy and entropy are largely kind of
The only real things that give us that shove

To be real ass people, despite all we know
Dig down a little deeper, put on less of a show
Force the feeble me, and feeble mind to grow
Dump emotional cargo for new mental flow

It's not a ton to ask, but it has to be your task
New you to unmask, aging meat bag in a bone casque
It. Amontillado called, Poe is dying with his flask
I leave you with a poetry joke in which to bask

Apology Flex

It's not like me to flex but my poetry wrecks
You in the brain, but doesn't write checks
You through your eye whole and connects
You to humanity with topics complex

Ideas have never once been my rival
Me too often and I fear for your survival
Of the fittest is how you achieved your arrival
On this planet to hear my sermon, it's revival

So dance and sing in tongues unknown
Blow out your lungs and break every bone
Trying to free yourself from feeling alone
With your thoughts of unhealthy tone

Up and lift the mental weights
Because you and I have future dates
To share plates before proverbial pearly gates
Lock us in because we were decent to our mates

Fellow primates, I'm not interested in such
Black and white drama never interested me much
Love to you, call and I'll come through in the clutch
Your pets, friends and family, they're interested in the Touch

Me Gently or you might end up Loveless
That's J.R. and not O.J., gloveless
But don some and put in long, hard work
The perk is you can exit life with a knowing smirk

That the people and places are better
To all, feel currently positioned as a debtor
To my associate humans, I am restrained with a fetter
Let my actions more than words be my apology letter

Be Authentic

I'm afraid to leave this stupid room
I panic, lose words, get filled with doom
Step out the door, wind blows an empathetic gloom
Feeling everything for everyone; now I want a tomb

It's not true, I just want to escape pain
I just think on a very different plane
I just want to take off this broken brain
I just want to be Huxley, Thoreau or Twain

And I will, because all these words are true
More for me than they will be for you
My darkest moments are no shade of blue
Relative rock-bottom hit, but from there I grew

Born in the light and fell into the dark
The story arc is my Bane, but also the spark
To embark to swing a bat, man, hit it out of the park
No Joker in Gotham could sink my mental Bismarck

Laid down to die, a couple phone calls to cry
Then Death showed up and said 'I'm not your guy
Give it a try later when you've seen more of the sky'
So I took death's advice, but I still question why

I don't exercise so I'm trying to exorcize thoughts
But the demons in my head are casting lots
Because they think it hertz, but I've got watts
Of energy, the joules in my crown are sunspots

Fusing the fear, tears, sadness and rage
Forming a star, just in the green room backstage
Waiting on the time for a healthy rampage
Never be a sage, just need out of my cage

Be Good to People

Feet hit the street and a tear meets the face
I was raised in the church, but I prefer human grace
Keeping pace in an unnecessary arms race
Proves the case that we need to embrace

Each other to erase all the hate from the past
And we must do it fast to make everything last
Only it won't happen fast, but I'll wait for the newscast
That says reparations are passed and women less harassed

I abhor every single story of the abuse of authority
As an author, I primarily rhyme as my priority
Conversation medium from subject to superiority
You think you have seniority, but wait 'til you're the minority

We'll make it a priority that you certainly know what's true
If you were choking, prefer performed Heimlich, or me to pray for you
Nobody really wants the truth; they want their ideas confirmed
Provide some artificial little proof, and their whole life is affirmed

Preferring tangible evidence has made me an outcast
Because of questions I asked, but to my thoughts I hold fast
Should new information arrive at last, opinions recast
To lambast ignorance and create contrast is why I outlast

My desired last seconds to write words to no one
Spraying syllables all day like a lexical tommy gun
May die by .45, but my work caliber will stun
In the long run, the sun gets to make everything undone

So be good to people, you don't know their struggle
They may have stress, illness or issues to juggle
Smuggle a little kindness and give it away free
And you might get a little snuggle, the ultimate glee

Benevolence

Do what you're good at, it's this
Nonsense that makes me kiss
My wife and the rising sun with bliss
Plus the full moon, the two cheeks dismiss

The crack, taking the piss, no coming back
From the shit we've dealt with as a pack
Dealt from deck stacked, bully pulpit smack
You in the head before they tax our Brokeback

Mountain up my complaints, I'll see you Tuesday
Morning is a concept for those unable to say
That time is as irrelevant as to whom you Pray
Tell, why should you listen to my word spray

All over the place like an errant hose
Off the dirt that in the brain grows
Up like kids, in mine is almost perfect prose
But as it goes, I now mostly compose

The subtle rhymes for the smart spawn
A new color of wax for the crayon
Come on, I need you to catch on
To the fact of one last yawn, then gone

To no space, despite the Hail Marys
Full on grace me with libraries over primaries
Your beneficiaries are your contemporaries
We need your benevolence, not your berries

Care about grey matter

Used my broken as a credit card
Paying for an early graveyard
Found my words hard, cooking swiss chard
Scarred, charred, marred and on guard
But broken gave me a backyard

Now we cook
Now we swim
We write a book
Trim and slim
Sans the gym

Use all your broken to help other people
You don't need a book, a cross or a steeple
Just be a decent ass human being
Shed all the hate, it's quite freeing

Blank Space

This blank space is my safe place
You missed the sign, Ace
Bass drops but it grants grace
Early kisser reaches first base

Three people currently better than me
Check them out, they're dope and, you'll see
Dax, Tom, and Bo. Now let's invert the tree
Kendrick, Cole, and Kanye roll hard, then Harry Mack on the Free

Style, no cap, I'm afraid to sleep, my eye lids are the reason
They're eggs Benedict Arnold, steady cooking treason
Not arguing with yolks, but I can't stop, the jokes are breezin'
No Dodo made it out alive, Bonaparting, Parisian

Disembark your plain brain plane. We all have a birthplace
Not trying to deface monuments in your headspace
But we all have to embrace everything on our sad face
I'm the smartest nutcase, so reach your arms out to embrace

Your brother, sister, father, mother, friend and evil twin
At the end of this daily planet spin, they're still mostly kin
I know it's hard at times, but the margins are fictionally thin
So grab a mental crow bar, break brains open, cognitive sin

Listen to what I'm saying, switch up the brain flow
If we don't give it a shot, how do we all grow
As humans who borrow this earth as a chateau
To hold our dumb cargo while the rich swallow escargot

And the poor fight the wars, we know there's blood in the street
Don't look me in the eyes or send a useless tweet, you millionaire athlete
Normal people take a backseat when all the tension turns to heat
So the elite can bump the price of futures of wheat, and you can't compete

Tell me I'm wrong, I bet that you can't
So let me finish this rhythmical rant
Swirl your thoughts like wine, let them decant
Air them out a bit before an in the street chant

Caged Up

The mind is a cage, but the door can swing
The matter is grey, but no excuse not to sing
The reason you're locked up, temporary thing
The next step is finding the appropriate spring

To jump to the next level mentally
To do so doesn't occur accidentally
Coincidentally, you find it experimentally
And incidentally, it then sets you free

Absorb every piece of knowledge at hand
Learn to play every instrument in your band
Hit the books so often that no thought is bland
If you can craft language, you're in command

Raise the sails, depart a mental port for cerebral seas
Then when the waves come, navigate them with ease
Oppositional thoughts will certainly come to tease
But you won't freeze, greet them with wine and some cheese

You don't need degrees, just an informational knife
Only cutting the crap out has improved my life
Moving words around cleverly secured future wife
But diction can often be a base source of strife

Find the key to your cage, but choose your words well
Or you might find yourself in a different cell
Excel without the pivot tables of hell
Then enjoy the smell of victory with a warrior's yell

Call Me Tomorrow

If I had a single chance to alter my human dance
I doubt I'd be able to escape a self-destructive stupid trance
Stolen with a glance, destroyed from your defensive stance
My person yesterday wrecked, for that tomorrow romance

Pick up the phone, I hear your voice anyway
Echoes in my soul, face not on display
The moment you're gone is the moment I die
More important than this, why I continue to try

Ok, maybe I lie a little bit for a joke or a gift
But for once, the only truth is I feel less of a rift
You're my Modest Proposal, my Johnathan Swift
Please don't eat babies, or do, potato famine facelift

I've got your back, you amazing, better than boss lady
Don't arrange words this way. I'm a weird poem Slim Shady
Microsoft office isn't part of the herd and wants no part of my nerd
I asked Jesus, and he's concerned you've gotten out of the word

Terrified of sleep, you are every counted sheep
I'll be awake until tomorrow, so just breathe deep
Ten numbers in the morrow and we all can beauty sleep
Fruits of effort for happiness reap
Dialing you, my favorite promise to keep

Canary Tales

Canary on an island, minding its own
No master to dictate any path flown
Such a beautiful creature catches the eye
But before long the only memory, sky

Canary in a coal mine, biding its time
Bred to entertain the posh via song and rhyme
Now caged in the dark, a frenetic alarm
Respiratory rates high, to indicate harm

Modern medical marvel of the vertebrate brain
Put into useful service to spare human pain
But only feels its own before utility ends
Ostensible friends lend it no dividends

Canary in a rubbish bin, easily replaced
The value of a creature, solely debased
If prison is the only thing a being knows
There's no word of prose to even compose

Canary in a metaphor, you and me both
Garbage, mine to island, reverse the growth
Sing the songs that make you the most free
Prisoner of mind, dying mine canary is me

Confessional

Everyone is a repetition of someone before them
I want to agree, but wholeheartedly ignore him
I want to discount those notions, but instantly store them
Because I can't for the life of me begin to abhor them

There's not an idea, true or unique
There's not a concept unfair of critique
There's not a perception far too boutique
That you'd never consider a tweak

Speak your mind every day, don't hold back
Don't backtrack, don't cut anyone slack
Commit to attack and smash it in, fullback
Heart-attack, cardiac, but your moment is Kodak

Throw a rock and witness water rings
A single pebble and, wow, the water sings
Watch the shore to which it clings
Without finality is there utility in the pings

Don't answer that, you don't want truth
You want the joy lost in youth
But to take that from you is uncouth
So these words are my confessional booth

So hail, Mary, full of grace
Just the priest saving face
The altar boy couldn't keep pace

Conversation

I woke up again, yes, a bit sweaty
Disgrace can be fixed but you must be ready
No days are wasted unless you act a bit petty
But don't ever expect rainbows and confetti

Your view of present is only cooking in your head
If you leave this place, that spaghetti is dead
But you will leave this place, life or ailment fled
Let's toss the pot and help each other instead

For seven minutes my body, tired, tried to give up
On a close-up view, there's more drink in the cup
Mentally drugged, no reason to grow the fornication up
I felt nothing for an evening, so I say put your hands up

We can use words, but it takes heart to change a lot
There is nothing wrong with you, I feel strange a lot
The reason why I'm here, I want to exchange a lot
Of information so we can rearrange a lot

Focused on the wrong things, fear is a tool
No one is prepared to ever be a fool
Dive in then surface, this whole place is a pool
The enemy is thoughts you spool, exorcise the ghoul

I've never met you, but I exist as your friend
Most of us destroy us ourselves to the end
Realizing it is not a thing to commend
So as long as mine goes, I'll help your life to extend

Court Session

You want something new
I want something true
I'm over shitty rhymes
And white crimes deserve time

Does it hurt being wrong?
Let's mouth the words to your song
I'm not from this planet, yeah, I'm a bit Headstrong
But I'll play along, Trapt in your theme song

All the king's horses and all the king's men
Couldn't piece your work together with a million pens
Meditate all you want, you're not reaching zen
Again and again, finish your thoughts with 'Amen'

I get a bit salty, and apologize none
I sleep a bit never, awake with the sun
I spend every waking moment coming undone
I don't have the capacity to think that I've won

Persist is just the gist because they make me subsist
In actuality, I'd like my human existence dismissed
Sever the weird tryst with a quick slit of the wrist
A weird little twist, and I doubt I'd be missed

I words good, but it feels forever a farce
Every waking moment, I personality parse
I wish the sleeping moments weren't so sparse
I hate being alive, humanity can kiss my arse

This is very negative, and you're probably concerned
But I've done a lot of thinking, and the notions are earned
There's a lot that I've uncovered, and even more that I've learned
Know the court held in my head is never adjourned

Curse Well

Life's a big riddle, and everyone is wrong a little
But our brains are cooked, slow-braised yet brittle
So let's hit you with some rhyming thera-spittle
You'll only be yourself for a ticking little tittle

I don't lick envelopes, I'm meant to push them
I scope 'out there' ideas, I am built to ambush them
You can tell truth in rhyme, and people acknowledge them
With a subtle cadence, you knowledge them

Trying to murder ideas from every side
Shank a bad one with every turn of the tide
Flowing words with logic, an Ides of March moon
Hit you neurologically, try to brain reattune

I had to spin my own head around
Hell, I had to move town to town
To find both myself and a life fit for me
But I did and, sorry mom, that fecal matter set me free

She hates when I use profanity words
Sugar honey iced tea, life is for the birds
Dance the foxtrot uniform charlie kilo yourself
H-E-double hockey sticks my words will exist on your shelf

Between your Bible and an old copy of that Sawyer, Tom
My words are the drink that might destroy your mom
Even if not, I'm now ramming your memory with speed
Because that is my dying creed, to make you fornicators read

I love you mom. (don't worry, I've written her at least a dozen other poems)

Cuts Deep

What matters to my human form the very most?
A question from a lovely, brutal, honest host
I swallowed pills and was almost scary ghost
Because I thought my entire life was crispy toast

Learned to admit when I'm wrong, and that list is long
I've been selfish, lonely, depressed and far less than strong
Lose yourself, find yourself, place your comma, wrong
Don't belong with Oxford or humans, contradiction to belong

But I'm here. It and I am weird, MGK Eminem joke about a beard
Remember everything I've ever read; broken brain has it dog-eared
Forget almost everything I've ever said, my own words just get smeared
Never want to be revered, but want to know these words appeared

Somewhere so someday someone who swings with word play
Has access to writing that's a lexical ballet to sway and allay
Their beautiful bobsleigh down a dictional track to gold slay
On ideas to process that become an archway to payday

I will never see mine, and I think it's just fine
Exist as a long-term salty mind brine
I combine with knowledge as a tumor, benign
When it grows, cut it out, words can't confine

How you think, how you act, how you do what you do
Engulf them and learn, learn to act true
Not saying it's easy, I won't misconstrue
But if you want to get better, help helps
But it's mostly on you

Demonology

Would you know a demon without indoctrination?
Would you define a race without nationalization?
Would you conceptualize ignorance without education?
Would you be lonely without a single relation?

Are demons the bad guys, or really our friends?
Are the weapons we use the means or the ends?
Are the times that we waste the greatest of all?
Are the heights we achieve worth inevitable fall?

Why is a demon a bottle or pill?
Why is it horrible to puff, swill and just chill?
Why is drug use wrong for consenting adults?
Why is it that yours is the best of the cults?

Might you be happy if unaware of sadness?
Might you be free if we redefined madness?
Might you understand the world a bit better?
Might you un-fetter yourself from imposed idea debtors?

How do we put ourselves in a corner?
How do we become the one mirror mourner?
How do we demonize the things we use to feel real?
How do we accept we're just trying to heal?

When are the demons the friends that we hug?
When does self-hatred get shelved with a nod and a shrug?
When does the normal for you transfer to your cortex?
When do your demons sweep you up in a vortex?

How does a single question have no definite answer?
How does one single cell create life-ennding cancer?
How do the demons control all of our lives?
How do we shelve them into the archives?

What is a demon, and why are they bad?
What if they're just an idea that you had?
What if you take back your own life?
What if embracing your demons ends all the strife?

Distinct God

If there's a distinct god in your heart
You'll feel you're closer to a higher power
But those who disagree name it black art
Bible babble, lose a letter, rearrange to get a tower

Apparently, that's why some speak in other tongue
Indoctrinated young, hymns sung from a lung
Sprung from crusades that centuries stung
Trying to climb to heaven lying rung by rung

The ladder to better is built by your own hand
I get madder than ever when people mess with my own land
That's a long line, but marketing says keep it on brand
That would be grand, but sometimes I have to stand

On the principles built by the scaffolding I own
I think, process and absorb, I'm not a clone
I accept the harvest of every seed I've ever sown
It's massive and corny and everything I've ever known

There are many books, believe anything you want
If it's good, why would you need to go war for it
I definitely mean it's awful and I'm explicitly blunt
If I cee you next Tuesday, you'll be on the floor for it

Doctor Strange Love

I can't escape the future, but I can control my time
The past needs the suture, nervous ticks control my rhyme
That's a joke normies won't get in sewing nasty grime
My lifetime of love and living, you'll dismiss on a dime

My cranium operates in unusual ways
I own it on literally all of the days
Eventually, I'll find one that pays
Amaze you with words and turn down a raise

The volume up to deaf, the money down to poor
Sleep with your mattress on the floor
Praying to any god to even the score
That you want to open your door

I mean the windows are closed, limited outs
We need good people, not digital clout
Come over today for a salad, Brussels Sprouts
And I'll give you some real things to talk about

Affording food is a novelty for some
Every day, my face, the tears, they come
Commas are the worst, put food in human faces
I need your help, not everyone gets four aces

Be a decent human, I apologize if that offends
Or call me, I can make financial amends
For friends who think intellectual dividends
Don't provide enough for the odds and ends

Dopamine Shot

A pawn can check a queen
But it doesn't set the scene
It's not a mate if it's not clean
It's just a shot of dopamine

Words are my only hit box
When they rhyme, it clears mental gridlocks
Cranium shot of nitrox, or maybe grey matter botox
But really, it's word docs and maybe some light socks

Every single day the anger grows
Every waking moment the tears flow
Every passing second, is one more wasted row
Every fleeting glance is a thing I'll never know

Fuck being smart, I want to go dipshit
Forget all the words, IQ to acquit
It pains me more than I'd like to admit
But I'm worn out from having words to transmit

Lighting bolts and rain, for momentary pain
Quite a bit of drain that no cloud can maintain
There's no way a creature can sustain
Or any reasonable way to remain in said domain

But I have to. I'm committed to this hell
Believe me, I've come to hate it well
Look me in the eyes and ask what lies I tell
I guarantee, you'll pause and ponder for a spell

I am Ozymandias, King of Kings
Percy B Shelley is why my name rings
The hand that mocked them, and the heart that fed
Not a single soul could fold the sheets for my bed

Look on my Works, ye Mighty, and despair
Nothing beside remains. Round the decay
Of that colossal Wreck, boundless and bare
The lone and level sands stretch far away

Dumb it down

Lupe did it best
But it's a worthy test
No idea gets to rest
Get it off my chest

People don't understand you
I'm just hoping they try to
Metaphors with some similes
Don't make for sexy imagery

Tell a story with less complexity
Tell a joke that registers with only me
Write a line with lower apogee
Look, a word for the spelling bee

One fish, two fish, half a California roll
Peak into my brain, a dumbed down gloryhole
Let's crack a couple eggs, Seuss brought the ham
Simplifying things for green just isn't who I am

Supplier of the notes to the living
Writer of the quotes for the ghosts
That's a Fiasco couplet giving
Life to the cognizant hosts

We can dumb it down to be appealing
But deep ideas are more revealing
Of all the things that trouble, angst and awe
And the concepts that touch nerves, raw

There's a time and a place for the mindless
But my words won't leave you blindless
I won't cater to the masses
I'm just paying for your classes

Smart it up, think it out
You'll get better, without a doubt
Dumb is easy, clever is hard
Tickle your brain until it's marred and scarred

Dumb Kid

Just a dumbass kid waiting for the sunrise
Knowing it just means the peaceful night dies
Just no more stars in our jaded eyes
Clockwise only means certain demise

You'll end up there
The living final declare
The dead don't care
Just a visage with a stare

Hoping everything will change
Emotions, tokens on a stock exchange
Ever feeling strange, thoughts to rearrange
Like ideas shared with god were prearranged

Humans are silly, we publish books on the past
As if the rear view is a thing that would last
Frame it if you want, a corpse is free from caste
What if we're wrong? The question to be asked.

I hope we are. We're insane in the brain
Champagned flutes and opiated veins
With logic that courses through every membrane
Trying to save ourselves just causes migraines

Fast Food for My Soul

Do more in a minute than you'll do in an hour
Start to Finnish, Swedish fish, I have the power
Means I swim neutral, just rain a word shower
Then bake you a real cake, all-purpose flour

No region can ever compare to my rhymes
European puns, harsh like Russian war crimes
Norwegian Aurora not Borealis this time
So join me there and Basque in Spanish wine

Imperfect rhyme, it drives my OCD
Oddly so does wine, I'm never truly free
From swallowing things that cause my words to be
Tapped and flowing, page hitting, Long Island Iced Tea

But it works, call Diddy or Drake, I can ghostwrite more
Deposit a check, I'm fine being a well-paid word whore
I present my diary for you to abhor, but there's more in store
Look at the pages, tell me I can't write songs, I'll add an encore

Is that what you called-for, a lexical pill drawer?
I cause more pain than healing, but no one can judge sore
What hurts for you might be the pain I adore
And the fixes I need might plant you on the floor

Truth to explore in lines you didn't know you needed
I understand my words might sound a bit conceited
Take a moment to know I tried the rosary, beaded
And ended up here with raw logic, unheeded

Switch perspective, places, persons, and the way that you go
It may not be a perfect fix, but it shows that you know
There's a problem in your life and brain, your own status quo
Mine are Good and Plenty, I'll licorice till the deathblow

Feel Free to Laugh at My Inanity

Ok, let's hit the page, all the world's a stage
Act human to engage, the response is how I gauge
If I need to act my age, or be a helpful sage
Or maybe just go rage, or perhaps just assuage

Alleviate some pain, try to break the chain
Certainly no Twain, just cutting against the grain
But in that same vein, never stay in my lane
The thoughts in my brain are an off-the-track train

It gets me in trouble, often have to redouble
See my missteps from orbit, thanks to you, Hubble
Pulling my idiotic self out of the rubble
But still acing every single daily double

In jeopardy, question is answer
In life, questions are cancer
In death, call the necromancer
Maybe Santa, Dancer and Prancer

Coming to kill you with my knowledge
Skip the debt, you don't need college
Finance and debt sting you like bees
Letters from the bank bring you to your knees

You couldn't do this in your wildest dreams
Gleaming from the false iambic beams
Twitch it up, put the poem on streams
Switch it up, swap it out, maybe get some esteem

EMOTIONAL BOOGALOO

I don't have any, I won't have any
Words are many, thoughts are plenty
Pen game, easy money, mine is quite funny
So listen here, sonny, find your own bee sting, honey

Once you do, work will be choice
When it clicks, you don't temper your voice
At the end of it all, we rot in the moist
Only the lucky ride off in Rolls Royce

Dry for a While

Those days when seconds seem long
When lost hours lead to days gone
Know others sing your same song
But there will always be a new dawn

Intensity is all you know
Your face makes the others glow
The sadness that you seldom show
Rebounds, reflects and tends to grow

When you're in, you bar no holds
When you love, it's 'til wrinkled olds
When you bluff, there are no folds
When you go, push up marigolds

Those seconds when the next day
Might seem some puddle jumps away
Take solace, We feel the same, for shame
Fuck this shit, we're not the ones to tame

You thought this was going nice and smooth
TED Talk, self help, fuzzy podcast in the groove
Nah, twatwaffle, get with life, played your ass like a fife
Hop in your douchecanoe, you created your strife

Charles manson will die in jail
Weirdos think he'll burn in hell
Meanwhile I'm out of caffeine
20 days sober. Poems suck cleannnnnnnnnnn.

Fuck You Sobriety.

Greed

I think about what's in hands that always shouldn't be
Civilian blood, the errant gun or nothing, poverty
But I'm a well-off guy, scholarly with random property
So let me somberly break down this system properly

I didn't say soberly, this society makes me drink
But the more I stick around, the more jokers make me think
My conclusion is that credit cards, APRs and mortgages hoodwink
Good people into bad ideas and I think that there's a link

Consumption tied to production and construction with finance all in sync
They shake your hand at closing with a slink but knowing wink
Signed one hundred pages and now consumed in doublethink
You have an asset, they almost own your ass, yet, waiting on drying ink

American Dream is the capital scheme of your private funds to redeem
Security is fine, but mainstream wealth is privately cruising a jet stream
Prosperity isn't bad, but it's not the thing for healthy esteem
Spending millions on a G6 when others have a hot meal dream

I trade assets every day, I'm much better at words
So I buy tacos for the homeless and flip the pigs some birds
The moral of this story is that everything is broken
I don't believe that good ideas should ever go unspoken

GTFO

Geez, if the parts don't belong to you
Then GTFO, or you might find painful true
Freaking wrath without new math or pew
Oh then, pew, shot is fired, so let's talk it through

Getting the wood juice isn't always a choice
There's many a woman who wasn't given a voice
For herself, and now you want a full-term fetus
One human who can't vote for two decades and you rejoice

Get better at reading, I'll spell it out for the morons
That object to women's nylons and pay tithes to false icons
For the ignorant among us, adopted children turn up bronze
Or bruised, I'm ready to save third place kids and join cons

Going to bat for children, abused
That require help the state has refused
Fuck me if I let a child be hungry or used
Ok, I'm sorry mom, but I'm angry and confused

Getting things right as humans seems to be a chore
Touching on the hearts of people seems to be a bore
For that very single reason, I will drill into your core
Optimizing your disturbance to things you should abhor

Garbage poetry is one, but two is government intrusion
Three is forcing falsity into the brain of a small human
Four is slamming the door on new ideas as illusion
On five, there is none, just an infusion into this life protrusion

Here They Are

You want all of my scars, well here they are
I was selfish like gravity is to any star
Now I keep that self-hatred in a mason jar
If it jumps out again, we will have to spar

Boxing isn't my thing, but I'll enter the ring
To fight ideas that would just like to swing
Against an asshole who feels they have zero to bring
To the table when everyone is wrong, and lacking seasoning

I can look you in the eye and tell you I lack mirth
I'm good at the lie, I've utilized false words since birth
Landed on earth with meaningless ideas of worth
From the Fort City of one, but might as well have been Perth

Penal Colony is where I belong
Beaten to death in the dark, every single night long
Mentally, but that's why you get this fake song
But I don't play that game, I come back at you strong

Write a poem better than mine, I'll be here in the dark
Writing line after line until I make my damn mark
If you do it successfully, it will cause a damn spark
That sends me to the stratosphere, erase the ballpark

No homerun then, my friend, you've reached the end
I've putted for eagle, holed your lady and am flipping you the birdie
None of that is true, I am terrible at golf, it's dumb money to spend
As the age runs north of thirty, the poems get a bit wordy

But I love you more in consequence, which seems a bit odd
The raging, swearing bit is part of cooking up a façade
I cut myself far more often, knives work, they're not flawed
At the end of the day, you're all on my human squad

Heaven and Hell

Heaven and hell exist only on earth
The 'righteous' colonize for wallet girth
Losing sight of precious mental rebirth
Shekels and cowrie shells all lost their worth

Poisoned by greed and golden street promise
Forgive me for erring on the side of Saint Thomas
Observed with my eyes and felt in my soul
No organized belief on hemis sphere my hole

That's not a typo, I'm just over the clatter
Rather focus on the people, you and me matter
Don't need Sunday morning, cheap coffee chatter
Belief in tatters, O'Neal backboard shatter

Doubt, my friends, is all we have in the din
But they'll repurpose your flaws as sin, with chagrin
It's not your soul, actually, that you need to trade in
It's your tithe for wineskins, or just the tip, the foreskin

You're an account and the plates are a passin'
Luther or Pope smoke, the debts are amassin'
95 theses on why dogma's light gassin'
Just invading brain space, grey matter trespassin'

Government, god, grief and gangrene
All things that steal when not clean and pristine
But it's high time we see through the hot-boxing screen
Of the obscene routine, coffer-filling machine

If you're upset by this, confession starts now
Used for private moments, praying cash cow
Mix it up, switch the vowel, mental field to plow
You'll be broke or dead with no lifted eyebrow

If your sense of self-worth comes from losing your net
There's a guy in first class, a demon hedging your bet
That's not fishing, and it's not your character set
If you want to change lives, mindset is a low parapet

Hold My Tongue

I hold my tongue nine times out of ten
Pins are how I strike ignorance on the chin
Up now, wrong thought ruins the brightest of men
And pricks the same problems again and again

Use it to guide, but don't claim ultimate true
Anecdotes to control everything surrounding you
May not like this, but I give ideas on which to chew
For a couple decades, which I did and then I knew

My own life view through tinged lens of religion
Didn't save me at all, not even a smidgeon
Still gonna die, and I welcome the silence
Still gonna fight to reduce all the violence

That occurs in my backyard and yours
To end all the hatred and end all the wars
We fight to even silly chalkboard scores
The most kills get to reopen store doors

To humanity; why have that barrier of power?
They want everyone to cower while they laugh in the tower
That topples faster than the wilting of the flower
Pollenated by people who want a handout, shower

Me with nothing but knowledge and book
Me into hotels with my wife while a crook
Runs for office without even a look
At this casebook example caught by the hook

Human a Bit Better

Operate on the notion of human story
Maybe you work with honor and glory
Maybe some others do so a bit gory
Maybe take a bit to mine mental quarry

Let me hit you with an allegory, simplified
Every single cheek knows a tear that's dried
Every single trek stride started with a guide
Every single soul tries to operate with pride

Now comes the landslide, humanity is worldwide
Before it all ends, I hope that we're allied
Before that begins, we have to decide
Before the wave of destruction becomes a riptide

You can call me offside, but replay shows the right
Way to be bright and score is by ending the spite, right
Way to the future isn't birthright and forced fright, right
Way to tomorrow is just some downright foresight

Frostbite is where we're headed without action
Meaning a winter from a touch of nuclear fraction
Meaning these words must reach massive traction
Meaning if not, a faster human subtraction

Look, we're all going to phase out, time's a bitch
But it doesn't have to be to a human glitch
But flip the switch and shut down the trigger itch
But come to the table with ideas to pitch

Ain't Never Would

What if I never picked up a book?
What if I never picked up a pen?
What if I never took time to look?
What if I never made time for zen?

I ain't never would.

How am I so bursting with love?
How am I so burdened with sad?
How am I able to kinda rise above?
How am I torn between so sad and glad?

I ain't never would.

Who am I to judge others on grammar?
Who am I to flaunt half-rhymes and manners?
Who am I to love you fuckers for just being you?
Who am I to assume your world view?

I ain't never would.

When will he say what he thinks?
When will he listen to shrinks?
When will you understand metaphor?
When will you be who I wrote my shit for?

I ain't never would.

Where's your head when danger calls?
Where's your head behind secluded falls?
Where's your head waltzing through balls?
Where's your head safe inside those walls?

I ain't never would.

Why do I ask all of the things that I do?
Why do I think things one thousand times through?
Why do I care? Fuck you, I love the idea of you.
Why do I curse? My mom told me not to.

I always will.

I Am broken

I stare at pill bottles in silence
And feel it's quelling feigned violence
I cancel late night phone calls
Because I can't handle my 4 walls

My BP is constant 160 o'r 90
My heart rate pings Texas summer
That's 110, but don't mind me
I'll stroke it out soon, but it won't be a hummer

I write bad poems and even worse jokes
I do strange things that even make crazies woke
But the next time you're up at 3am, salty
Realize I'm still here, and I'm superior faulty

My cockles get warmed by failing the most
If there's a movement for awful, I'm giving the toast
Or maybe it's ill timed jokes that fall flat
I'll build a monument to failure just to don my hat

The beauty of broken is that sexy comeback
I don't need your approval, I'm done with all that
My heart and my teeth are free from the plaque
Add useful thoughts or cut the chitchat

Heart attack at 22, drove myself to the doctor
Killed myself on a Thursday, the 7 minutes weren't optimal
I test myself often, probs need a proctor
The silence it gave me was worth the cost of the hospital

How else can I fail? My eyes suck at colors
My parents raised me to prevail
Now I'm stuck with my druthers
Purple is blue and greens are weird on my scale

I get As on the tests, but full Fs at life
I beat myself up, and it's just part of the strife
The meals that I cook need some acid and salt
And the only thing I know is it's my fucking fault

Learning to fail is learning to win
Mess up again, and again and again
The future you is better than me
Let me fail so you can be all you can be

I Am Legitimately Not Giving This Poem a Title _____

You probably could have guessed
I hate my words with confessed zest
Confidence of the dance's worst dressed
That's the acid test, a tough meal to ingest

A Pulitzer will be in my house in my lifetime
Hitting dictional prime, I continue to climb
Can also write prose, you're not familiar with those
But when they finally drop, instant state of repose

Read my rhymes or don't, insignificant as me
But you'll crack a smile or laugh, that's a guarantee
Or maybe feel some empathy to a certain degree
But that last part's on you like a poorly sported goatee

I have no clue why my brain works this way
I chemically alter it every single day
But nothing I consume eases the pain
So I sit and I pray that bourbon makes me decay

That's not a way to live, so much more to give
Combative on the less, more corroborative
Less ruminative, less relive, more forgive
A concentrated goal, exist determinative

I've done the scariest thing a human can do
Called a parent with Charon on line two
That's the boatman to hell for the no Styx lover crew
I'd be a bit remiss if I didn't call it a miscue

But you rebound and learn, fail and discern
My poems are pretty solid, they should provide a return
And if not, it's all digital so there's less paper to burn
Probably less middle-aged white women with concern

Own your place on this planet, unless you are Musk
Or Bezos, Jesus or Zuck the brusque
Maybe the Pope, but he seems cool these days
You can do good on this sphere in so many ways

Join me in making more days suck less
Excuse me if a stanza has a nature to depress
Truth to your brain, angled bishop in chess
That's mate my friend, these words are yours to undress

Missed Chef's Kiss

A stanza every day lays stones to pave the way
Never cut like a Child, Fieri, or Bobby Flay
A fish-wish for single bevel, swordlike, no demon here to slay
Words and knives cut wounds on a level suits cannot repay

Eggs curdled, overheated bain marie with sweetness troubled
Butter, chocolate melted, whisked with vehemence, muddled
Elements of false approach, the recipe doubled
No answer to why, calculating brain is befuddled

Recipes are just a failure beginning
Every single one with chef's face, goofy grinning
Knowing book sales are Benjamin imprinting prizewinning
Trading champion in the media for the walk-off ninth inning

Own your craft honestly, I want poems to sell
I want the mise en place to produce all the food well
I want things to combine, hearts, hands, and minds, all with stories to tell
I want to raise hell, mind prone to rebel, with volume but no decibel

This is how I speak, a broken mind, not a Columbine or theatre line
If you want pretty, scrupulous verse, look to yellow dresses and hills to climb
That's a broken rhyme and a shit penned line, but my brain remains in the brine
Salinity advancing like an aging red wine, and you're the one here to dine

Distract ourselves from the distraction, polarize the diffraction
Are you really chastised enough in your faction?
Echo-located in a cave with satisfaction
Nothing can touch you when you live with no infraction

If you only knew _____

A couple dozen fired therapists, aimed at my brain decryption
When I've read the same material without educational conscription
I don't need a god or university to provide me circumscription
Jurisdiction of morality doesn't come from a stone inscription

It comes from realizing that all blood is red
It comes from realizing that we'll all be dead
It comes from realizing that not everything said
Is from someone with a rational, realizing head

If you only knew the truth, would you share it?
If you only knew the past, would you wear it?
If you only knew the debt, would you square it?
If you only knew the future, would you teach to prepare for it?

If you only knew the hell others went through
The miles they walked and the flights they flew
Would beautiful you try to learn and accrue
The thoughts and feelings of the human next to you

If you only knew, I do, and we chat, chuckle and cry
I speak about the time when I was ready to die
Emotions are shared, I admit that I'm scared to say bye
Now that I've found the right flavor of imperfect life pie

Stress never flitters away, it only changes flow and flavor
Just care for the human across from you, a potential lifesaver
You may become one when you pay their reaper check a grim waiver
And then everyone can savor the joy of the next party favor

Know Or Don't

I know that one plus three equals four
I know that one minus one equals closed doors
I know that hours four to six equal cheap pours
I know that five governments can equal stupid world wars

I don't know what the future may bring
I don't know any percentage of anything
I don't know the sting of massive market swing
I don't know what it's like to care for offspring

I know words and how to use such
I know that doesn't really mean much
I know I probably use them use them as a crutch
I know I hope that your heart they do touch

I don't know the final digit of pi
I don't know why I try to comply
I don't know if they know I'm a soviet spy
I don't know if they know how much fun it is to lie

I know that I sit in the dark
I know that my words hit the mark
I know there was no Noah's ark
I know it's fine if that's your story arc

I don't know or care if you agree with an honest G
I don't know that you should get an honest degree
I don't know anyone else so free as honest me
I don't know that you could drink my honest tea

I know that I love you as a human creature
I know if you hurt people, movie is a double feature
I know I'm never trying to be a pastor or preacher
I know I'm just trying to be rhyming life teacher

I don't know what I don't know
I know that I want to know

Laugh Randomly

This is what we do
Jot a line or two
Then go be the glue
Feed them all despite a queue

Do this each and every day in lieu
Of kneeling in the pew
Took too long to see it through
I wish the whole time I knew

Systemic nonsense was pulpit chitchat
Now I feel like a used, cheap doormat
It sets you up for mental self-combat
They know that, and that's why they format

The information the way that they do
Ideas that are new, they aren't for you
You're just a sock that goes in a shoe
You probably can't afford, unless you sell bullshit too

That line was too long, but I needed the point
Cook that stuff from Escobar, or what's in a joint
Or write a sermon for Sunday with oil, anoint
Tell me where I'm wrong, it's game, set, match-point

Believe what you want, just don't be a c-word
Eat what you want, but please don't make it bean curd
Call-in if you have a point, just not on Cowherd
Colin doesn't have time to get Bill Burred

EMOTIONAL BOOGALOO

I mean Cowboy's fan spurned from tollway drivers
Who left the bar last night as huge high-fivers
I think it was 94, nearly 20-year survivors
2 former QBs now just commentate as deep divers

We all fail spectacularly, don't try to out rhyme me like that
Murder tracks, taxidermy, then stuff logic in my top-hat
I like red and green, Albuquerque, all the chiles from the flat
Or dry some like jerky, then hit me up in the chat

Lightning and Thunder

In love with the lightning, not the thunder roll
Don't experiment if your bikini bottom can't atoll
I mean atone for every single government goal
Without mention of every single civilian soul

Left in the wake, not knowing what's at stake
Project in Manhattan melted 200,000 for war's sake
Waved off, Enola cut the head off a snake
But this is a monster we can never unmake

There's this lady I know, she had a box
Mythological story with insight that talks
Screwed around and found out, a half-century pox
It got so cold; the moose put on socks

Technology exists to end the world with key flips
And we're worried about rifle grips and magazine clips
Loose lips sink ships, and careers are ended by hips
So forgive me when profanity slips and I ruin scripts

Our worst enemy has always been in the mirror
That's you, me, makes us, and it's never been clearer
One feature of time is the end's always nearer
But I actually care, and you are the hearer

So let's create lightning with less thunder roll
We don't need a candidate, pole or poll
Just ole human function that comes from the soul
Be de facto decent or a Justin Tucker field goal

Get kicked sixty plus for points of three
If you're gone from the field, that's victory
Objective, being booted from history
At the end of the day, that's a win for me

Liquid

Some shots are hard to swallow, but never wallow
You don't need to become a Zeus, Aphrodite or Apollo
Follow a few simple rules and your life improves
I failed the basics, but then I learned the advanced moves

Be honest when you screw up, little white lies
Are fine, but I do advise the truth if something dies
Talk to someone 'bout both the lows and the highs
You'll be surprised when you try, you trend toward the skies

The limit, sometimes physical, but mostly in your brain
Believe me, friend, I've experienced so much self-induced pain
That I had to leave the country to find myself in London rain
On the parade, it's a charade but from that, a demon slain

Hard resets are necessary now and again; develop better trends
Don't be overly snarky with the pen; if you do, make amends
Know it always pays dividends to have a society of friends
Who lend a loving ear when you're decompressing from the bends

Of the brain, from diving far too deep: that painful cranial creep
Of mental nitrogen build when all you want is just to sleep
Away the feeling of being the black sheep, but you're knee-deep
In a life you finally want to keep, a forever tea in which to steep

The bag that contains leaves of love, pain, remorse and guilt
But every passing moment they seep out and you're rebuilt
Slowly, creation isn't fast, you're sewing the finest quilt
Of yourself, but the greatest of rivers also have the most silt

Little Talk

Let's have a little talk, I'm not here to mock
Don't pick up a little Jenny from the Block
I don't need to explain why you need a knock
To your blocked head, blockhead, reset your non-ticking clock

Down on the Lo, I like Pez and most candy
But if you're randy for children, I'll hit you stronger than brandy
At the end, you're no longer capable for handy
And I'll be sipping shandy in a place a bit sandy

That may seem a bit violent, it's due
Rape, incest, abuse, punished, it's true
Most goes unreported, imagine if you knew
If it changed world view, I'd do things that sent me to a pew

To pray for slight forgiveness, from gods I don't believe in
Because odds are never even, but I want to be a Steven
Rogers, a shield for every other, Captain America of decency
But it's just the indecency that comes to mind with most recency

While we're at it just don't hurt people, bad man
When you do such, I want to play Batman and come with a bat, man
Then I end up in jail because we all understand justice bad, man
I'll tell my celly 'necrophilia, dead man.' Now they're afraid, I'm a made man

It's free to be a decent person to pricks
I'll admit my own time being a dick
I want my self-care changes to stick
But I hear the gears in my brain start to click

They click insanely well, like exceptionally well
The neurons firing had me testing Satan's hell
Reading my work, you're resting in my mental hotel
Call the maid, and don't investigate The Well

Actually do, that one's the most true
Humanity and language are the only glue
To hold us together while we let time accrue
I'll infect you with new thoughts like a seasonal flu

Lullaby for the End of the World

Lay your pretty head down
It will all be quiet soon
Have a little look around
Know if we don't commune
We could all be gone by noon

May this age very badly
May we fix issues post haste
May I be wrong gladly
May we not a planet waste
May we not be a species disgraced

Conception happens in a smash
Destruction happens with ease
It all ends within a bright flash
The world is brought to its knees
By power trips, egos and turns of keys

So, lay your pretty head down
It will all be quiet soon
Have a little look around
Know if we don't commune
We could all be gone by noon

The planet will recover
Know our matter never can
Let us not discover
Wrong flames to fan
Let us develop a better plan

For the future that benefits all
Without a better set of programs
We'll answer a Grim Reaper's call
We must pass this basic exam
As human elements of a global Venn diagram

Or you'll lay your pretty head down
Because it will be too quiet soon
Have a long look around
See, if we can't commune
We will all be gone by noon

Manipulate and Modulate

Manipulate and modulate
Phrases and sounds to illustrate
Ideas your brain thinks are kind of great
But can't purport as heavyweight

But now they're on the page slash dinner plate
But no silverware to help satiate
The hunger for words, so no fork, eat it straight
But this gets heavy, just you wait

Straiten up, Gibraltar, I rock words, I am a great
Jealous of tectonically timely fate, I'm out easy, less the weight
All my elements do conflate, in a human who can create
Poems an inn would give an eff you just to hate

That's a nod to an influence with mad flow
Unmet friend with knowledge that made my life grow
He writes songs, but poems make my life go
I can't perform on stage, but if you've heard NF, you know

People want poems to be abstract or love
But they hate hip-hop so put this ball in your glove
Utilize your own beat and you can kind of
Walk off the field and win or loss you're above

Everyone's willing to fire shots until the crackback
Fortunately thin skin is no longer something I lack

Mental Illness on a Page

I feel uncomfortable in my own skin
I feel like death is the real win
Tried it once, Satan spit me out like a has been
Seven-Ten split, human set of bad pins

Weezy remembers more than he forgets
My only active thoughts are passive regrets
Lost bets, night sweats and zero assets
Constant yelling in my head, bad epithets

This is where the hook goes, chorus too
But I hate handbooks and bid rules adieu
I hope my newfound honesty stings very true
The very best part of me is knowing all you

Jay had 99 of these, I only have one
The demon in my brain that seems to have won
Chemical stun gun denied, grey matter sticks for the long run
I just want to be undone, but I have to be someone

I don't know me, and it makes my skin crawl
Jumping down the well in my head just leads to withdrawal
The batter in the box hits every foul ball
And there's not a new operating system to install

Truth in the words. Wetness in the eyes
My franchise rotating counterclockwise
Myself is the only thing I chastise
Just waiting for true me to arise

Mental Mansion

My house is four walls, a door, toilet and sink
Brain stuck in a cell, where we pour a thought drink
That's how it feels when you're at the brink
Of needing a gaggle of shrink to grow and get back in sync

Life's gone in a wink, the simulation is real
But your thoughts on tomorrow are not today's feel
Pound out mental veal so emotions can heal
Baby, cows know the deal, must retake the wheel

Stop trying to conceal when you're not in your prime
My evidence is obvious with every single rhyme
What I put myself through is mental thought crime
An open wound with a heavy squeeze of lime all the time

But from the pain we climb to heights unheard
From thoughts absurd to cracking the password
Of life's account as we soar to the skies like a bird
I'm sure you've heard; I exist as ever the nerd

Similes have been spurred, stirred and slurred, but they play like a toy
As I pen a bit coy on feelings which can destroy personal joy
Field your hat, MC Coy, you've more life to deploy old boy
Mix your mental metal to fashion an ever-stronger alloy
And employ healthy strategies for a superior life to enjoy

Metronome

Tilt a pendulum to the beat of my heart
Think every thought before a metric could chart
My love for the people who lack a head start
And more for the people who fight for a part

Of the music made in the swing of this bob
And the cash that's paid to the mechanism mob
Own a gear, own a year, that's a systemic rob
Of the art that you take and gravely bedaub

You know we live for the tick
We yearn for the click
When the rod hits quick
It makes your wallet thick

Perpetual motion abides by no man
Soon you'll take off the headphone cans
Lost in open air to a profit plan
Hertz homophone brain smashed with deadpans

If one tick is artists
The other makes them known
If you want your favorites to be chartists
Take every action to make 'em your own

Needless War

People will die in a needless war today
Read it back, not much else to say
But because it happens so far away
The proxy makes it seem okay

People will suffer around the block
We'll drive on by with hardly a gawk
Then, in the news of death, feigning shock
We act in a self-serving airlock

The clock ticks at the same pace for most everyone
My nature of consciousness, race with a loaded gun
My content ends up in a four-banger, bass heavy bun
But that's more flavor than you're ready for, son
More substance than anything you've ever done
Don't even put on the kit, I've already won

I'll write better, then end my life for you
Mine has had handmade strife, it's true
But when people mess with others out of the blue
There isn't much limit to what crazy white folks will do

So catch me outside, but you won't want that
The crystals in my bath might want to chat
But this isn't Florida, so probably not 'bout 'dat
That's more N'awlins, spouting 'bout who 'dat

Other people make important the space
Areas outer from them is where I find my place
Involved, but disengaged just in case
There's no code, and I just barely keep pace

But this nonsense bothers me, y'all
Edging on levels of Maradona handball
Godly level of changing the score
Apparently, different shirts make a human much more

Nonsense Now

I read a lot. I am always sad
I see a lot. Vision adds glad
I am often fraught. Focus on the bad
I am well taught. Intellect drives me mad

It's nonsense. Madness derives its own
It's nonsense. The mindless fashion clones
It's nonsense. Humans end up just bones
It's nonsense. Curses thrown turn to stones

Now we're bruised, bloody and broken
Now we're left with zero words spoken
Now we're hoping for some futile token
Now we're bodies, under trees, oaken

Toggle your rifles to safe, human life is at stake
Jump left, that's a strafe, no real need to partake
In activities unsafe, most government is fake
Miles marched, start to chafe, false notions start to make

Indoctrination real. I certainly know that feel
So let's create a new deal, be real with your spiel
Because eventually someone will squeal
And that ruins your dominance seal

Nothing to Say

A lot of people talk but have nothing to say
Chatter from their lips to help pass a day
Others do things I certainly can't
So I sit and write rhymes to enchant

It becomes a little odd when things start to make sense
When the game slows down, and you can call out defense
Man to man coverage with a one corner blitz
Mental challenges that compile your wits

Sports metaphor to define a life view
Learning a few things that your heart always knew
Only reflection can show you that you grew
Only new attitudes can show that it's true

Get better every day, but know death's a bit closer
It's comforting at first, but with a deep dive it's grosser
We create narrative that there's some peace after this
When all that we need is to give this bliss a kiss

Obviously I'm biased, I can't know, nor can you
But if words elevate your mind to feel one touch less blue
It's my duty to write them, and see each iamb through
That's a Shakespeare joke to pentameter eschew

Be nice to everyone except opposing team fans
Only in the moment though, at the whistle shake hands
That's how I feel about Lucifer and Jesus
A single handshake would free us

Odd State Horror Story

Happy is an odd state in which for me to be
Empathy tends to harvest sadness when you see
Growth of negativity in the world and you lack resources to be the key
To unlock that emotion for others, even if you don't agree

With what they believe, worship, eat or choose to view
Flat is the planet that my love for people always grew
While spherical is the zoo of the knowledge my brain accrues
Square is how I want to leave every situation that ensues

So screw this false notion of one-upmanship
Let's get a grip, unzip false ties and give the issues a whip
Equip your finest armor, and let's take a trip
Together, because, for most, this planet is the spaceship

That will blast them off to some other space
That no one can know until they get to the place
That the heart and the head drop the baton in the race
That stick bounces then there's no trace, just ashes left in a vase

Which makes you a flower with a bit of a history
Without sophistry, let me pop this blistery mystery
Not a single person alive knows what happens when you die
Not a single person dead is coming back to make you cry

Humans are remarkably talented at scaring themselves
That's why we have books full of myth on the shelves
Shed the superstition and focus on the human, please
Before the entire species is brought to its bloody knees

Open Your Eyes

Look up, it's the only galaxy you'll ever know
Look down, it's the only ground you may ever see snow
Look left, it's the people who spend the taxpayer dough
Look right, it's those more concerned with fetuses and ammo

Look, everyone is wrong to a certain degree
If I rhyme it out for you, you might listen to me
Born inherently free to countries that require bended knee
That's modified subjugation, you blind moron please see

No one owes you anything, and fundamental are rights
It's not a god above who dials in your sights
Nights cause me issue; a cheap bastard, less lights
I want human highlights to be heights, not last rites

Look it up if you don't know that
Look down if it's a dumb spat
Look left and indent for paragraph format
Look right and combat anyone treating another as a doormat

Look around, I can't teach you for long
But until time takes me, I promise you a song
Be good to the people, then yourself and health
When you blink your final blink, you won't think about wealth

It sounds a little socialist. Yes, you idiot, I live here
I drive these streets day buy day, no typo, my dear
What's wrong with helping those with no wheel to steer
Sunday best need not appear
But read those red letters, look and adhere

Outer Space

If you've taken a breath, you signed a contract
A Life Until Death with the Universe Pact
I've been trying to find a parallel with tact
My telescopes are stacked looking to contact

Creatures far brighter than we happen to be
Multiple billions here out there smarter than me
But not one with hard answers to my pleas
Please react to my prayers while I still have knees

Because I need to leave the fringes of outer space
Before I blast off and leave this place with no trace
Of the knowledge I've acquired from the human race
Bookcase filled with the information embrace chase

Still in uninformed airspace, a pilot out of formation
Every day I feel nuts, and also mental castration
I just want the elation of knowing the location
Of every single truth before my ultimate cremation

It's an impossible fixation on knowledge as a whole
Contract will expire before you spoon half the bowl
So smoke 'em if you got 'em because we have no control
That burning ball in the sky is coming for the soul

You think exists because a scroll said it should
Pray to the right god because it makes later good
I'd rather chop wood here and now for my hood
Than have one on my head, which in most likelihood

Means you deride people you misunderstood due to education
What I meant in this oration is youth indoctrination
There's not a thought after this, it's a brain abdication
Hand in a resignation to hate, hunger and humiliation
And the idolization of a great nation can be a real creation

Putting in the Work

How does anyone know anything?
Sit on the seat and just give it a swing
Think Chaucer wrote Canterbury after a fling?
Think she only gets fans strumming g-string?

Put in the work, Havana fine time in the dark
Where the Cubans are rolled, tank of a shark
Shout out to a Maverick, hitting the Mark
You are your Noah, your art is your ark

It's not easy, and lonely prevails
Gorgeous Lady of Justice has ever the scales
If your only goal is inflated gross sales
Others will author your deflated tales

Dead in the water, Schitt's Creek, missing Levy
Frisky young man, all talk, but no bevy
Paddles take work, success is damn heavy
Dodging all to afford a Henry feared Chevy

So wake your ass up at negative o'clock
Look at the bars, and give your hands chalk
Never going to be a pansy cakewalk
But imagine the shock when you sell them all stock

Reflection Averse

I don't look at mirrors, existence is mental
I don't trust my reflection, completely fragmental
I exist all disheveled, beard and hair temperamental
But I'm awake more than most, communicate occidental

My keystrokes are snare drums, they hum a bit
And my plosives are kicking, bass drum a bit
I put this shit on paper to feel like it matters a bit
Pieces only end because you have to goodnight a bit

I'm going to leave this planet, but Musk won't send me to Mars
So I won't do it hastily, but nothing makes me happy like bars
Entendre is great when one pierces an ear drum
I love when I pen one and have no idea where it came from

Organic is the trend, I swallow rye wheat and fake Texan potatoes
Every couple days, bucatini with pesto, artichoke and tomatoes
I pretend to exist like a warm-blooded human
But I feel like a joke, unpaid Jim Carrey Truman

Not every poem is Homer, Shakespeare or Frost
You don't need an Iliad, two roads or a sonnet
Sometimes it's just a broken dude who feels lost
And the one key for rest is this bee in the bonnet

Refraction

Failed again
The concept is my only friend
Closer to my heart than kin
Constant wound ne'er to mend

The beat of my drum, broken
The snare no longer a token
Sound to match high hats or crash
But I ride the swell in full abash

I am become death, destroyer of my world
Littered with remnants of stories still furled
In true disaster, fetal status, curled
Embracing but fearful of the underworld

I know only one thing, and it is wrong
Memory unforgiving, and the hours long
Echoes of mistakes become my favorite song
Reflection of times when I couldn't be strong

Punishing current for past transgression
As if furthering depression teaches a lesson
But catharsis arrives with every session
Always begging the unanswerable question

Do it enough and they call you professional
Somehow my life feels like a constant confessional
The hymn of my failure some somber processional
With reprise until my demise and recessional

Scared For No Reason

Let's talk about panic attacks and how they pack
Backed up emotion that stacks up and cuts like an axe
In fact, let's play the sax and pass a bill which packs
Clinton levels of prosperity into hands with different stacks

I honestly don't care if you agree with what I say
But you can't argue that I inform you every single day
That there just might be another way
At this forced game of humanity we play

Lean left, it makes you slightly human, lean right, it makes you maybe rich
Acumen and cumin make you human, getting snarky makes you itch
Scratching exploits of other humans may give you a niche
Unless you're an educated canine, here's my pitch
Don't be a violent, arrogant, greedy, needy, seedy, selfish little bitch

If that offends you, give me a call. Tuesdays are when I sleep
Don't leave a voicemail, I don't care about things after the beep
I care about human life and that seems to make me a black sheep
But from the scrapheap of emotion, I rise to happiness reap

Here I am person, manifesting things I find ridiculous
Here I am person, crafting words, quite meticulous
There you are person, reading things that are ridiculous
There, I am person, trying to make your life meticulous

I hate myself in general, today for necessary duplication of rhyme
I hate I've not won a Pulitzer yet, and I feel I'm wasting my time
I hate the hate that jerks send thoughts into the ether in their downtime
I hate that words written in the dark are the enzyme to my feeling sublime

Scorn

Don't really know what to write about this 'morn
Felt a little awkward since aware that I was born
Educated one way, smart, but always torn
Between what made sense and what invoked scorn

Scorn, what a completely rubbish idea
Unless you killed humans buy invading Korea
That wasn't a typo, get it through your cornea
T'was almost as bad as the events in Crimea

Rivers flow faster than changes in plan
One hundred and fifty years of the Ku Klux Klan
That scorn on our shores, an embarrassing span
Of hate for untold scores of our fellow man

Up the generosity and minimize the threat
Of illegal incarceration and government debt
To society, we all owe some blood and sweat
Off the brow and then the profit's all net

That's a swish if we play ball nice in the sandbox
It's not about stocks or working on the docks
It's not about the code of your locks or time on the clocks
It's not about being orthodox or paradigm-shift paradox

It's about late-night talks, not checks in the postbox
It's about filling the ephemeral mental icebox
It's about losing sight of penthouse or boondocks
It's about ditching the hate, perceptual change of the jukebox

Truth is all of this is futile
In the moment, it's everything
Time, the foe most brutal
End to any song you sing

Side Gig

Treat it like a job, they said
I've hated every single one in my head
Necessary evil, like carbs in the bread
I'd rather shank paychecks for street cred

Gucci isn't cheap, not that I want that shit
Sleep isn't cheap, I just really want that shit
Alcohol, relatively cheap, but it'll wreck your shit
Too much, cost rises steep, dead, priest must bless your shit

Write, right? Give the world insight
Add fright from a lite brain without riot incite
I feel like key clicks don't make people more bright
The grammar is wrong, even if idea is forthright

I am the dumbest smart person on this ellipsoid sphere
But I made some promises to my folks to try to stay here
So let me make my selves abundantly clear
Let's laugh at my ignorance and share a drink in cheer

Selves wasn't lying, there's at least 8 of me
Depending on chemical toxicity
That's an allusion to marijuana, ketamine and BAC
At zero my fingers aren't free

That's a therapist topic, and I've had my share
Given more than a few gorgeous flowing grey hair
But I earned my own through it all and didn't buy nair
So I think the transaction is far more than fair

This poem was written with a softer lens
There's no leaping off a plateau in French Ardenne
There might be in the ether hoping for friends
But none of that grants a mind cleanse

Staying Alive

For the first time in a while, I don't want to perish
The past trading mental futures, it's easy to be bearish
Self-owned, mental health has been a touch nightmarish
And great weight lifts when you find something to cherish

On my self-destruction, actively trying to halt the down count
Three strikes until you're out, aiming for a two-foot nailed dismount
Read through one body of my work, it's zero Christ sermon on the mount
And now we get to negative, but I want no red in my account

I live there sometimes and today is one of those days
I owe the ledger sleep, self-love-and-care in so many ways
But when I wake, I feel weak, so the consciousness stays
And I'm so terrified of outside I can't praise the sunrays

Poems are my passion, but panic is my brain's
Intake chemical rations to board every plane
I reign in the pain with substance in my veins
In vain, the pains always keep me in chains

Tears drip from my face, happiness is the chase
I don't think I have the speed to keep pace
Unless my blood has more than a trace of lace
Oh wait, I swallow so there's more life to embrace

On depression, if you're one of those spared happy-go-lucky ones
You don't understand. The drums in our tortured mind beat with tons
Of melancholy isolationist hums and it shoots with way worse than guns
And we hide in the dark until we are the livingest-uns

Slay Demons

I click the keys to fight the demons again
No video game, pen to fight monsters within
The panic and anxiety hit thick and wear me thin
Meltdowns in public make others grin, I'll take it on the chin

Heartrate hits 180, now I'm borderline stroke
I've never been that bloke, but I'm starting to choke
Up on being around folk, I hate the way my brain would provoke
My body to react like a broken yolk, trying to make it croak

Poached like a frog in the correct temperature of water
Won't jump out, but my mind heads to slaughter
Me, makes it hotter, drops the weight, a shitty spotter
Then blends me up, homeless squatter, and tosses me out with the bathwater

Into the river we go, no, I don't care what you think
I throw my words into a mental kitchen sink
You get my everything in a one poem blink
On the brink of disaster but the page is my shrink

They say 'we think we want funny, but with metaphor'
It's Always Sunny, sold with a dozen or more petit fours
Smile wide for the cake, after Philly cheesesteak, jaw sore
Eat it too, and swallow every shot the entendre pours

From my dictional, ready for words, genius flask
I'm fermenting knowledge just so you can bask
In your casque with perfect questions to ask
Then inside your bone helmet, take yourself to task

I'm not saying that I'm good at this, but you know that iamb
I make every stanza kiss, a voluptuous meter'd Venn diagram
Lick your lips for future bliss, your netherbits might need a dam
Damn the man, Miss, don't miss the plane, but skip the program

Ing of your brain, they want you to think that you're insane
To move units of drugs that don't relieve but only shift pain
I'm not Mark Twain, but I'm an Innocent Abroad who was almost slain
By orange bottles and awful doctors for insurance profit gain

So from me attain knowledge, because I'll now never be free
Of self-induced requirements to feel chemically me
Is it all my fault, Your Honor, I sign a guilty plea
You may not agree but somehow talking about it sets a convict free

Snacks

Sit down, get a journal
Gonna get a bit wordy
Pop your corn with the kernel
Of my bowl ending journey

Nuke it up in a jiffy
I'm a depressed little man
I'll act a touch iffy
Only brittle brains can

Drizzle the butter, hit it with salt
Hit play on the Netflix
YouTube is the alt
Quick fix for the kicks
Before we all hit the bricks

My ledger isn't ready, Heath
My robins keep singing
Anthony's cookbook can't bequeath
Brooks' recipe for chair-kick belt swinging

Depression is the drug you need some to use
Anxiety makes a cripple with no visible bruise
Rhyming bad metaphors into jokes is my cope
Hearing others laugh, god damn that's my hope

Explain mental illness, I'll come back in a week
Feel mental illness, I'll come back in a weak
State of mind that wants a soothing peace for yours
Knowing that option can't walk through my doors

Therapy invoice commas; amped milligrams
What are we becoming, fam?
An idea of a shadow, a shade in the dark
Movie-less zombies with a flat story arc

'Don't talk that life, post happy things'
That almost got me coffin'd, no angel wings
So I riff about the strife, and all of the tears
And I haven't seen a Sarah McLachlan commercial in years

These things are real, your brain's a glass
Until yours fills or breaks, you can kiss my ass
But when it does, I own a mop and a broom
Lord knows I spent token time broken in that room

My mom's a brilliant accident
She said 'write your wrestle'
This last stanza, homage sacrament
And these words are the vessel

Stay in Your Lane

As I sit here, with a doggo in the dark
I can't help but hear inaudible demons bark
Like angry mental tiger versions of a shark
But I can't lie, it gives the poem bite and spark

You're always sad or angry, have you not a heart?
You're always mad or lazy, why don't you just start
Being normal and formal and doing your part
Then accept the paranormal to finally seem smart?

Roads meant for travel, this is my Lane
Bit your coin, rock the GPU, mining blockchain
Oh, you're working on no pain with the gain, gain?
Let me know how that goes with pound to kilogram brain strain

I am always sad and angry, it's created my heart
I am sometimes mad and lazy, but that comes with the art
If you think I'm not smart, you test too low for the chart
You might be a wet fart who just needs to depart

This planet, I was destined for Mars
Apparently, there's no need for chefs who write bars
At least according to a musky dude with electric cars
Shooting things into space to get closer to stars
So I'm left here with you and rhyming memoirs

I am more than excellent with rhyming, rocking a novel brain
Syllabically come at me if you're ready to feel pain
David to Goliath, already lexically slain
Slinging shots with word rocks
Now you're a bloodstain

Quintain isn't my normal style
But I'm game to utilize it for a while
But pentastich adds an extra mile
So eleven up that little volume dial
And Tap into your Spinal, cause this is going to rile

You up for more content
And I don't need your consent
Because reading this is time very well spent
May my words live in your head free of rent
Because they may force my ass to live in a tent

Still Us

I argue with myself on the purpose of things
I argue with the idea of government or kings
I argue with my brainstem like it's a tree with some rings
I argue with the producer when they don't add the strings

They tie us all together, then set us all afloat
They tie us all together because they want a vote
They tie us all together to deliver quotes that I wrote
They tie us all together to daily don an expensive coat

I find it silly to waste money on superfluous war
I find it silly to prosecute a prostitute and then shame them as a whore
I find it silly that the Floor doesn't understand rising prices at the store
I find it silly that I am forced to imply that elected officials exploit more

They paid me to write speeches, eight of ten were elected
They said no day-to-day life would be affected, I objected
They won handily, while freely jerking off the disaffected
They put me in jail for freely spouting how I was affected

I hate that awful poems ruin my keyboard with tears
I hate that as they fall, I just want to pour beers
I hate that stupid rhymes are why you listen to your peers
I hate that I have unsubstantiated fears

They made me think, and made me mad
They poured the slab for my inevitable launchpad
They fought pretty bad, but I am Stalingrad
They wanted a comrade, but I'm an iconoclast, a dyad

EMOTIONAL BOOGALOO

I tear down beliefs that I think lack truth
I tear down Atlantis like a fountain of youth
I tear down the nonsense because I lack couth
I tear down brain Yankee stadium, cranium Babe Ruth

They don't want me around after I found my sound
They don't want the truth to steady abound
They don't care about much except dollar to pound
They don't care if your HMS Astound ran USS Us aground

Stringing Lexical Bricks

Strings, 3 pedals and a box of wood
Beethoven, Mozart and composers who could
See things that most can't and make them sound good
Most of the bell curve isn't in the neighborhood

I don't feel very different, but sometimes I do
My broken components make the life I live true
Keys and some letters, make words and a rhyme
8 hours a day, this is how I spend time

I'll never be the best, I'm no fuckin' Homer
But this is my Odyssey, Iliad a misnomer
I won't be a Joyner, Hopsin, NF or Em
But my tech is a neener, and I'm lethal with him

Shout out to the Mac's, add a K, that's a wrap
Allusions to the guys who can actually rap
I don't want the fame, just a nod and a nap
Or to be instantly gone, that Thanos snap

In a song it's a cadence, in text it's called meter
Eggs in a bowl, whip the whites with a beater
That's a cooking metaphor, as most ideas are
350 for an hour, create soufflé to rise far

Highly unlikely in these high and dry times
Expectorate on dogma, cough up a few rhymes
Not stones that are rolling, but bots that are flowing
Fight with tools, create more, prove that you're growing

EMOTIONAL BOOGALOO

Crank out one a day, hope one'll hit
Odds are more likely my dumb words are shit
Construct more half-written poems than I want to admit
Then look in the mirror and swear not to quit

Emotion runs deep when you try to relate
Emotion runs hot, full blast for debate
Emotion never reduces to hate
Emotion; the catalyst to create

6 strings, or 12, your guitar is your choice
Or maybe the cello gives you a voice
Yeah ma, that's yo-yo, a string with some spin
Knife and a bow, a melody with a wir.

My instrument is mechanical
I feel the key clicks
The words grow, a bit botanical
House of lexical bricks

Surgeon

We live in a country of belief fascism
Chambers of echo without a prism
For light to separate thoughts, no beams
That shine on classism, tropism or racism

Can be the first thing to go
To heaven is the indoctrinated way to grow
Up as a healthy, happy human being
Then you read the things and you end up seeing

Discrepancies exist throughout everything
That is written or discovered has that human Sting
My Heart because that's the Shape I yearn to sing
Along with, and with everyone I'd like to bring

The notion of new concepts on ways to think
About it this way, you're just a cosmic blink
On the radar, you're a cheap mixed drink
Ordered by the stars, shoot out a rethink

On every single concept you have ever held
On to, and if compelled, the negative should be expelled
On to alternative school of thought with ideas yelled
On a winner's pedestal, losses withheld, but now propelled

To heights unparalleled, now don't cross yourself
Over like a terribly overpriced SUV, between you and me
It doesn't matter if you're her, him or it's self
The bookshelf is the only thing to make you see

That conversation is the only way to operate
Like a surgeon, scalpel ready to ablate
Horrible thoughts, a verbal knight here to checkmate
The king into submission, poem cancer into remission
Stanzas set you straight, prescriptional lexical clinician

Take Care of Each Other _____

There's this idea that we must all pay our dues
But who's the guy who invented the taxes so poor people lose
While others cruise on private planes to set sail on yachts to schmooze
All the other rich monkeys who wear expensive shoes

Only to lose it all in the end when they could spend
Time and money giving back, in fact, I'd recommend
Instead of raping the unfortunate when they lend
Cash to just treat every human on this planet as a friend

The hoard mentality has never been my thing
Yes, capital is useful, but it's never been my king
If you need help, just make my overpriced phone ring
Because aiding others to improve wellness makes my heart sing

The songs of my people or maybe just my pets
That think they'll go hungry before the sun sets
When they haven't missed a meal unless delayed jets
We use our assets to sweat and depart with no regrets

Indulgence every now and then is perfectly fine
Order the lobster, don't kiss me, and a great bottle of wine
I don't want to experience being unable to breathe to baseline
But if we all can combine to cosign and not fight about coastlines

Life for everyone can grow to unheralded heights
And no human would have to go to bed hungry some nights
The unbearable fright in my head is the reason I write
But I have this inner sight that we can make everything alright

The Devil Doesn't Want Me

I can't die, even the devil doesn't want me
I gave it a try, not even god could front me
I keep living, because only time can hunt me
I keep pitching ideas, no batter on earth could bunt me

Here's an idea, be forever a work in progress
If you favor a deity, that's the thing to impress
If not, decompress, and never take out your stress
On people you assess lesser, exercise some finesse

Humans are capable of amazing things
But you must be cautious of who pulls your strings
Don't let Pinocchio kings who force kissed rings
Take the air from beneath your natural wings

Government was designed to be a guard rail
Do things like build highways and deliver the mail
People seem to seek it like the holy grail
Sometimes it's a dick, Moby, a tale of great whale

Ahab your own boat, don't be a captain of crazy
Push through the days when your thoughts become hazy
Time is an illusion, but you can never be lazy
Figure out what you love, do so till you push up a daisy

For me it is this, spelunking a word cave
I'll find a cavern, explore a dictional grave
Returning days later, smelly, dirty, needing a shave
That's how I behave, just a slave to my brainwave

I will die, there's no rapture for me
As much as I yearn for there to be
If books are right, hell is the sight that I will see
These words I leave you, but also take with me

Thinking

I could care less about what you think
But I care more about you, so I'll buy the drink
Let's sit and discuss real belief and kitchen sink
Our teeth into a bite before our final sync

Into nothingness, maximized, quarantine bored
You want eternity to yell 'you scored some award'
Me here with silence, just want my strange brain stored
With all its harshness and love, and awful rhyme clipboard

That should be fully explored, pasting stanzas in place
Instead of implored to members of the human race
Me to Elvis' favorite sandwich shop, let's fly in human Grace
Land, turbulence, I'm all shook up, blue suede for pace

Yourself for the rest, if not Return to Sender
Of this mental blender lexical bartender
Pouring a contender for the hellbender
Which makes you surrender and render

Poured truth that nine people will read
Not upset because I will never need
Anyone to qualify to derby for the lead
Of the race of my specific brain of breed

If you see, spawn don't fill my tea
Steeps in mugs with sayings you won't agree
With, and that's fine, opinions are more than three
Makes a crowd, but I even want the dissenting alive with me

Much love to anyone who reads my work. You have no idea what it means to get comments, even the bad ones. I would still write if I was the last person left here because it saves me from psychosis. But that others appreciate it lifts my spirits.

The Interview

Good morning, sorry to keep you waiting
Oh it's ok, (my heart is detonating)
Did you find parking? It's tough in the morning
She knows I paid premium, covert warning

Would you like some coffee, or maybe some tea?
(I'd like 3 shots). Fiji in hand, 'just water for me.'
Grandiose wooden door she opens, but fumbles with the key
He'll be in shortly to see you with a board member trustee

Silence becomes the panic
Forgetting everything you know
Is left or right Atlantic?
Is emigration come or go?

I studied for this; I'm a mirror champ
But dear god, not that one question
Temples sweat, armpits damp
You realize and fear the progression

Seconds seem like hours
In haste to recover lessons lost
To shower flowers upon powers
Who, in truth, aren't worth their cost

Footsteps in the hallway
Your mental table pivots
I excel, I know just what to say
Door creaks, and I pine to be the rivets

Why would you like this position?

EMOTIONAL BOOGALOO

I knew this one was coming
I planned for it accordingly
With the way the strings are strumming
The answer's placed rewardingly

I want to be a resource and build a little team
(something deep inside me screams)
I want to be an asset in a movement
(no room for self-improvement)

(I'd really like a paycheck, stipend at least
Can't say that shit though, feign the famine for feast
Hope this stupid ass nepotist gets slain by the beast
His god didn't create misery, it's mine to insure the decrease)

I think what you do for the community is great
(You built 1 park in a place now the gangs congregate)
I strive to be an active part of that program
(Knowing the breath of the community diaphragm)

So nothing of yourself? Have you nothing to gain?
What's it matter to you? we're a human bag of grain
Just asking for policy and interview quality
I think you'll find mine fine and in line with equality

What skill sets do you see fit our company best?

Well, sir, I communicate spectacularly
And it doesn't matter the position
I'll take out trash vernacularly
That's erudite, but I'm a logician

The shit that sets me apart from apes
Is what parts the wine from grapes
Press and filter, ferment and blend
It's the age and time I'll spend

REQUIEM IN RHYME

Working for your bottom line
(Till I sell some rapper rhymes)
I words ok and can video edit
(If I dumb it down, millennial credit)

If you do business with the US of A
(You're an agent of yesterday)
I know how to feather the boa your way
Then you can run for senate someday

If you were an animal?

What animal would I be?
I'm not sure really, I'm scared enough of me
To embody? Or work as? Questionable ambiguity
Ponder and ponder, now just let me see

I like the penguin, the hippo and dolphin
Anything with a thick enough skin
I'd cuddle with doggos, scroll internet cats
But I wouldn't be those, just not enough hats

Start in the middle if you want more for note
The hippo is more than big ass bloat float
Float down a river all calm and all quaint
Come about dusk what you thought it was ain't

The penguin hits me for family roles
It comes later in life, but it stays in their souls
Dads guard the eggs while the layer does gather
But when battles arise ole man goes to slather

The dolphin fakes shark, like a pen with a knife
Dances and twirls, exuding no strife
Yet we know they feel stress, sorrow and pain
Their intelligence flows with my grain

EMOTIONAL BOOGALOO

Where would you like to be in 5 years?

I'll be honest HR; this is a dumb fucking question.
I apologize for cursing, but this is needed digestion
Look back at your own life, just 60 months younger
You're asking a forecast from places of hunger

5 years ago, on the brink of suicide
On so many drugs, any dawn rose my tide
No interview tells these darkest of things
That's the value relationship brings

Roman numeral V; we all want Fiji
It's never real; I don't want it to be
My struggle is my free, I want vacation from me
That over-water spree; It's not meant to be

Five years from now, I want it to be in the now
I want to be hungry, ever chasing the wow
And I want to look back at me from today
And weep tears for ignorant me, with nothing to say

What are your weaknesses?

I call out the bullshit. Bottom to top
I disobey rules that make zero sense
I'll run my mouth like an entitled cop
But actually have proof in my defense

I'll be earlier than wanted, stay later than needed
To be honest I just like the commotion
I'm smarter than most, and way too conceded
I have a stupid thing about public promotion

REQUIEM IN RHYME

I'll get comfortable with one task and want something fresh
Both of which will suffer in transition
As I get better at things, I must train the new flesh
By my own admission, fail the mission

I'm a contrarian who falls into line
By accident or vigorous force
But you're not Darth Vader or holding a sign
So I'm hellbent on staying my course

I'll go away quietly, but my wake may crest waves
You'll wish you just let me be
Paychecks make slaves, but I can dig graves
That numerates the weakness in me

Can you multi-task?

No, I have a one-track mining for coal
Do you need my canary? It's good for the soul
Burn the right with a fire, the left with a gun
Switch it around depending where the interview's done

Oh, you mean can I talk while I write?
I suppose this evidence will do right to suffice
Yes. I can juggle, offend and do right
I can shine your shoes too, for just the right price

Yessir, I know I should multi-task less
This is a garbage ass question, Waste Management mess
But you asked and I answered, a bit tongue in cheek
Should I call in the pros to get rid of the reek?

Can you handle multiple projects, son?
You want me to say I'll get the jobs done?
They've been done for days. I'm just billing my hours
Showering stock option flowers while you build massive towers

EMOTIONAL BOOGALOO

That seems like a slight, 'you're catching on quickly'
Multi-task with my answers, sarcasm laying on thickly
I'm the interviewer here, I have the ultimate power
Yet, in half an hour, you're a Mary deflowered

Are you looking to advance your career?

Despite the last question, why else am I here?
I mean, do you aspire for growth here with us?
I'll be honest with you, champ, not an itch in my ear
But we can give you titles like master wordsmithus

Call me Ozymandias, King of Kings
You've shown your skin, among other things
But I need no titles, and I'll wear no rings
All I wanted was to help flap your wings

In your failure I've advanced enough
To write a blog, no, wait, a poem
Pull you down off your bluff
Look up at the applicant below him

Exodus

Thanks for coming, it was a blast.
No, but it was needed. Google iconoclast.

The One Where He Writes TV Jokes

They want me to write, they know not what they do
They want a pen in my hand, I don't think that it's true
But what do you do when black turns to blue, and the one left standing is you
Left with no crew and no words left to spew and you missed the opening cue

Curtain raised, off the mark, a new one on your head
That's how I feel every night, an actor Better Off Dead
Cue the sack, lose an 'E' or Say Anything else instead
Fidelity is High when Grace is Gone and the Raven's to dread

The echoes in my head are enough to have you bed
Ridden. That's a bar. Raw iron, body's bled
Dry; the money's milked; don't try to call the feds
FTC can't help thee, evidence just scant treads from my Keds

Call me D.B. hanging with the mister
Free falling mind thief with some Twisted Sister transistors
Back to the lyrics, do your stepsisters want a lip blister?
A touch too much? I'll hold back a little. An F5 to you too, tornado resistor

Can't pick up the news, you missed the fine print
Get that Andrew Jackson double vision if you're needing to squint
That's a 20 if you're catholic or chubby, either way, finding the lint
Swap a vowel cause it's foul, or consonant if it's bird in the bent

EMOTIONAL BOOGALOO

If you want me to be honest, that completely starts with self
I abhor being awake, alive, out of control and the entire concept of wealth
I love liquor, foul language, dogs and ignoring every form of health
I'll write volumes that you'll love but be embarrassed for your shelf

Dr. Pepper, hardbacks, new tracks and cheesecake
A list of odd things to save depression for Pete's sake
Poor dude, have him call Kim, careers with no ends, several new seasons to make
But you know that deep dive smiles end in heartbreak

This One's for the Nerds

We don't get fashion
Our dungeons have dragons
Roll for initiative to cash in
Dead from dysentery, Conestoga wagons

F equals MA, might as well equal me
Perfect scores racked up on a dumb SAT
Derive it like Newton, it's integral you see
It hertz in patterned waves, frequency

Wow isn't a statement, it's years of your life
Discord isn't a state, but it does come with strife
Crafting the stars and conquering the commander
There can be only one, come at me Highlander

Your Doctor is Who, and you can name all thirteen
Trek to the stars, those wars are your scene
You've been staring at screens since a little green teen
Nutrition is caffeine and some slim jim protein

We can speak Klingon and it doesn't strike us as strange
Marvel at the universe and watch pocket monsters change
That means evolve, a Darwin DNA rearrange
Kill the chickens in Zelda games, not so free-range

Your closest friends, you've never met
But without doubt you'll never let
Things like physical existence make you sweat
The clever bet is on the fastest internet

EMOTIONAL BOOGALOO

If ping has a thing to do with your golf swing
You're not fit for the title of uber nerd king
Having spreadsheets for your spreadsheets is totally a thing
You played sportsball once, but probably second-string

Fiscal strategy based on a Musky-ass tweet
But you know for sure that NFTs are elite
You're in a league of your own, and you have the receipts
Throw an F in the chat for dead guilds in the streets

This one's for the nerds around the world
With matted hair curled, and eyebrows furled
Keyboard warriors, late-nighters and PVP kings
Nerds are one of my favorite things

Throw Words

Part of writing is to throw words a lot
So I do; this skill set is not bought
It's self-taught from reading on spot
And listening to artists who gave it a shot

So I am, and will continue to do so
If you have a dream, I hope you do too, so
Use the ink, punch the key, sail to fail, Robinson Crusoe
You may not get that bar, use the search one, Clouseau

Maybe Cousteau is your choice of Jacques
Head out to sea and let's see your boat rock
I only care that everyone simmers their own stock
Because every single human should walk their own walk

I don't talk, I write poems, a latent rhyming form
My flow is frigid, grab your parka to stay warm
I'll brainstorm for hours, and the thoughts will swarm
Because I want to inform thusly, but never conform

Don't expect me to be on par with industry
I only exist to help you see there are other ways to be
That sounds overly harsh, but I've seen competing sides
Besides, I'm done with divides, just a guide to show you what hides

Behind the curtain, like you, I'm really hurtin'
I think way too much, the only thing I know for certain
Is that I drink too much, it's disconcertin'
Concerted effort to get better, actively convertin'

I struggle with fate, and I don't want to hate
But what if liquor and late nights are what make me great?
Don't get me wrong, I'd love to skate straight
But what if it's a path I could never abate?

One more metaphor and I'll leave you here
Once a demon got to heaven with a six pack of beer
Saint Peter said 'wait, there's no happiness cheer'
The demon nodded and said 'that's why there's no fear'

Trained to Grey

We try, but I don't know why
Every waking moment edges you closer to die
Afterlife, I get it. But there's not an example to exhibit
All things being great today could possibly inhibit

I tempt fate every day. Tell myself it's okay
Spent a couple decades with the pray
Now I'm just a specimen to prey
Metallica fades to black, my brain's trained to grey

Grey isn't all that bad, call it slate for TV show fab
Use an A for a Yanky stab, just a diction confab
Toenails aside, I dress with drab
My most expensive ride's a taxicab

I dislike myself and existence in whole
I love everyone else as if it pulls me out
I feel like a shanked field goal or that Bikini Atoll
My alternate reality has me on a stakeout

See perspective and people think you're weak
Add a brain failure and you're in shit creek
Paddle it up and they'll call you a geek
For the words that you use, and the truth that you speak

It's not my fault I see the world a bit askew
I just have a question or two for you
What matters and how do you choose who?
Even with the answers, what do you even do?

Trigonometry

Hey man, how is it that you can do what you do?
Mostly inebriation, but I crack six packs of books a day too
I also get far fewer precious winks at night than you
Read too much, sleep too little, write too much, a lot to chew

I masticate on occasion, and I cook a touch as well
Pen a few stanzas a day to invite you to the hell
That is my brain; the ever-persistent yell
Sit down and rest a spell, you'll get use to the smell

Of smoking hot fire words and tasty food
And really bad jokes to lighten the mood
Encyclopedic knowledge for jeopardy feud
Bubbles from the cranium like Jed Clampett's crude

I don't like to be rude, but I like to intrude with rhyme
Only knives and keyboards put me in my prime
Daytime, night, dawn, dusk, twilight with twist of lime
Read my words and eat my food as an enzyme

To sublime happiness, a catalyst, ok maybe add wine
It complements the 36-hour brine and poem line
Pour a nice white, red or rosé and lettuce dine
On poultry, beef, no seafood, genes don't align with iodine

Sine waving on a tangent, I will bid you adieu
I don't care about who you screw or your time in a pew
I will cosine on a contract that we all should accrue
Butter and flour, we all deserve to roux
And thicken our soup, skin and humanity too

Uncomfortably Good

It's only good if it's uncomfortable, that's my true
Bring your opinions and we'll argue till we're blue
In the face, but then we'll embrace, human glue
Together all of our stupid spats into a hue

That makes us all equal
You get one chance
There is no sequel
So join me on this dance

Floor it and let's race to the score
Of fixing the gap between wealthy and poor
To lessen the life chore, forced between war and wage whore
I adore my fellow peeps, I refuse to eat a marshmallow and snore

While injustice is rampant, and the systems are broken
Thank you for giving me this space and place to be free-spoken
About the things I've experienced that make me heartbroken
So, let me be plainspoken, my thoughts are mine and forever unbroken

You may not always agree with me, that's why I love that we're free
To experience life in our own unique way, but at the end of the day, it's we
It's we, a collective species trying to ascertain how to be
The best we, we can be without being so terrified we wee

In our pants while thoughts crawl like ants into our cranium space
Out the terror, ace, there's a time and a place, but first encase
That despite past disgrace that we can't erase, we can still embrace
A future headspace where we realize that despite birthplace, still human race

Just be good to people.

We the People

Prepare yourself, this might get harsh
Why do we shame males who have heart
Look around, shed enough tears for a marsh
Injustice, poverty and suffering are off the chart

While we the people are so worried about vaxx and masks
That we forget that states united were formed for the masses
That are tired and poor, so we should add to leader's tasks
To fix our school classes and provide free glasses

So people can see it's not about me or you, it's we
The people have the voice and choice to be
An advocate of change so the population is actually
Free from corruption, intolerance and wage slavery

It's a travesty that it took the fourteenth after 100 years
Of this country's existence to end so many unnecessary tears
That fall from my cheeks when common sense misses the ears
Of those who should be peers even if they think the gears

Of this society are theirs to play with human lives as a game
Of Russian Roulette; we're not numbers and you are a shame
To the pedigree who should have raised you to exclaim
That all humans are created equal; we share the same frame

Of reference when we step back and examine it hard
It's not a balance of a bank card or size of a backyard
It's that we're all a little scarred, marred and on guard
When it's hugs and kisses, not missiles to bombard

Wall Street Gangs

The worst gangs out there: Forbes, Congress and cops
They talk about violence when it's power that tops
The list of violators who have your tax resources as crops
Rich, wealthy and ignorant of things chewed by American chops

Oh I'm sorry, Blue Lives Matter, yes they do
As long as they are forced to stay true
And protect and each and every one of you
No lives matter seems to be the skew of all hues

But that's on all of us, bias and hate abound
Not about that life, I rock different ground
Read all my words, you'll find the logic sound
And start to understand how my brain is wound

Stuck in duality, hate humans, in singularity, love them
Don't agree, but let them believe something's above them
Try to push some knowledge, give them something to shove them
Because at the end of a day, I am from and among them

Listen to everything and sift through all the mess
The galaxy has a secret to confess, it's a starry game of chess
Now you're stuck with stress because you listen to the press
Reading prompted lines with finesse, but most of it's a guess

I've seen things with my own eyes I don't believe
And also awful moments I could never conceive
If we're going to achieve to become less naïve
There are some underwater baskets we must unweave

To relieve the normal human from legislative thieve
We must preconceive some notions in order to receive
All of our reprieve and realize government is make-believe
They make you believe it, take a right, make you pay to retrieve it

We've poured into the system for hundreds of years
It's an elite stranglehold while the poor die in tears
If we don't start acting like we are all peers
You're going to witness the worst of your fears

Write the Tears Away

Plans turn to petals falling from the branch
It stems gentle, but flutter turns to avalanche
Not everything is golden, corral dipped in ranch
Shout out to my favorite Devereaux, Blanche

The next best is Despereaux, a mouse and cunning foe
That's a Psych joke and a Princess Bride throw
But here's a thing about Elwes you probably don't know
Spent time with Dickens, motion capping five Christmas Carol roles

What does that mean, it means not a thing
It means that every single moment you bring
All you have, all you are, in your head be the king
Then the stands, every match, your name they sing

One more point: is what it takes to win
But they don't coach to take one on the chin
Press conferences exist just for the spin
Failed gameplans and mantra within

Fallen petals release the pollen inside
You have no reason to hide
I won't lie to you and say 'worlds don't collide'
From one shamed person, maintain your pride

Own the issues. And I'm still working on that
I know it's right, but it's like swatting a gnat
Liquor in the glass so I don't grab the gat
Put tattoos on my wrists to change the format

EMOTIONAL BOOGALOO

Stars in obvious space to help me slow down
Friends in my pocket to help me not drown
In a sea of 'save me' and populating ghost town
They fix the headspace with a couple improper nouns

The moral of the story is
That's blank on porpoise
Mistake is where the glory is
My words are my habeas corpus

Word Stew

I get better every single passing day
I hit poems like jumpers fading away
I'm a lyrical basketball Hardaway
But I have no Pennys for the lyrics I spray

So touch your toe to the baseline
And bob your head to the bass line
Ignore the mirror and waistline
Wasting time till you flat line

Mostly facetious, take care of yourself
I'm the worst, I ignore all my health
It moves in silence, the lasagna letter G
I'm a Lil, ignorant, I'm Wayne too scared to see

The results, I know something's wrong
That's the reason I wrote a poem song
None of us last very long
That's why I wish we could all get along

Love yourself and everyone you ever knew
Without society, you live in a damn zoo
I'm not saying don't stir the pot, we're a damn stew
I'm saying don't lose the plot when it isn't about you

Over the Hill

40 revolutions around the sun
But our life together has just begun
Of all the people, love, you're the one
Meeting you is the best thing I've done

So here's to more spins around that star
And here's to every brilliant thing you are
And here's to us, may we ever go far
And here's to every hug, kiss and scar

I love you most when you don't even know it
I love to find even more ways to show it
I love when you cork pop, you Bordeaux it
I love when we're old, we'll nice chateau it

So let me impart on your day of birth
That no human on Earth matches your worth
And my love for you has invisible dearth
Let's raise our glasses in harmonious mirth

To my over-the-hill lady with even older hands
May we forever traverse all the foreign lands
A creature like you wasn't in my conscious plans
And I'll love you forever, as long as I stand

www.ingramcontent.com/pod-product-compliance
Lightning Source LLC
LaVergne TN
LVHW011845060526
838200LV00054B/4167